FREEING THE FEARLESS U

A STUDENT'S BLUEPRINT TO OVERCOMING FEAR AND RISING TO NEW HEIGHTS

JASMINE 'JAYE' SMITH

Copyright © 2025 Jasmine "Jaye" Smith

January 1, 2025

Published by Final Step Publishing LLC

P.O. Box 1447
Suffolk, VA 23439
For Worldwide Distribution

Printed in USA.

ISBN: 979-8-9915622-1-8

TABLE OF CONTENT

"*Arise, shine, for your light has come, and the glory of the Lord rises upon you.*"

ISAIAH 60:1

FREEING THE FEARLESS YOU

THE STUDENT'S BLUEPRINT TO CONQUERING FEAR AND RISING TO NEW HEIGHTS

Congratulations! You're embarking on a bold journey to uncover the fearless version of yourself. Transitioning into college or high school brings new challenges, opportunities, and moments where fear may try to hold you back. But Isaiah 60:1 reminds us that God's glory is upon you, and you are called to rise and shine.

This program is not about denying the presence of fear—it's about conquering it. Fear can either hold you hostage or propel you into the destiny God has prepared for you. This guide will give you practical tools, inspiring stories, and creative ways to tackle fear head-on while growing in your faith and identity in Christ.

WHY FEARLESS?

Fear shows up in many forms: fear of failure, fear of rejection, fear of being different, or even fear of boldly living out your faith. Yet fear can become a teacher when we confront it with courage and God's promises.

Isaiah 60:1 invites you to stop shrinking and start shining. As a fearless follower of Christ, you are equipped to face fear with faith, resilience, and purpose. This program will empower you to step into the life you were created to live.

HOW TO USE THIS GUIDE:

This guide is structured into three sections:

PART 1: READY

You'll begin by identifying and understanding your fears. Through scripture and reflection, you'll gain clarity on how fear shows up in your life and how to prepare to face it.

PART 2: SET

This section provides practical tools and strategies for overcoming fear. With insights from the Bible and inspiring stories from modern public figures, you'll learn how to embrace courage and take action.

PART 3: SOAR

Finally, you'll apply what you've learned and step boldly into your potential. This section is about walking in faith, living fearlessly, and shining brightly as God's chosen vessel.

INTERACTIVE ELEMENTS

Each chapter includes:

1. Scripture Focus: A Bible verse anchoring the chapter's theme.

2. Public Figure & Biblical Inspiration: Stories of a real-world Christian leader or influencer paired with a biblical character who conquered fear.

3. Fearless Mindset: A key takeaway to shape how you approach fear and challenges.

4. The Challenge: A practical, real-world action step to help you live out what you've learned.

5. Fearless Focus (Reflection Activity): A journaling prompt, creative exercise, or brainstorming space for personal connection to the content.

6. Remember This: A concise summary to reinforce the chapter's key lessons.

LET'S PRACTICE NOW

Reflection Prompt

What is your biggest fear about this next chapter of your life? Write it here, and then declare what you believe God says about it.

....

....

....

....

....

....

....

....

Fearless Mindset

"I can feel fear, but I won't let it stop me because God's light is guiding me."

Challenge

Create a list of three areas in your life where you want to rise and shine this year. Share one of these with a friend or mentor who can pray with you and keep you accountable.

Remember This

A 3 POINT RECAP

1. Fear is not your identity—God's glory is.

2. You don't have to wait until fear disappears to move forward.

3. God has equipped you to rise, shine, and live boldly.

Truth is you're scared, just like me.

Completely terrifi ed that the world may judge you.

Because all they see is someone trying to be
Little Mr. or Misses Perfect
but they have no idea that it is impossible for you
to make earth fit
into your impeccable design to be original.

The world will never understand it,
so instead of wasting your breath
to compensate for their inability
to see the real you and me,
choose to be fearless.

EXCERPT FROM THE FEARLESS POEM
BY JAYE SMITH

CHAPTER 1

TURNING SETBACKS INTO SUCCESS — OVERCOMING THE FEAR OF FAILURE

AFFIRM IT

"I embrace the challenges before me and trust that every setback is a step toward the success God has destined for me."

SCAN TO VIEW VIDEO

Failure often feels like a dead end, but in reality, it's a pivotal stop on the road to success. This is a truth embodied in the lives of both ancient biblical characters and modern influencers who have transformed their setbacks into powerful stepping stones.

Let's explore the journey of Kai Cenat, a rising star in the digital world, alongside the biblical figure of the rich young ruler, whose story reminds us of the courage it takes to prioritize faith and purpose over worldly values.

KAI CENAT: A MODERN TRAILBLAZER

Kai Cenat is a millennial influencer who has captured the hearts of millions with his humor, authenticity, and work ethic. Recently, Kai broke the world record for the most concurrent subscribers on Twitch, solidifying his place as a leading voice in the digital space. Yet his journey to the top wasn't without challenges.

Kai's early life was marked by financial struggles and uncertainty. He faced doubts about whether his unique content could gain traction in a saturated online world. For many young people, the fear of failure—of putting in effort only to fall short—is paralyzing. Kai's story shows that overcoming this fear requires grit and a willingness to take risks.

After achieving his monumental victory on Twitch, Kai's response was one that defied popular culture. Instead of focusing solely on self-promotion or material gains, he publicly praised God, celebrating his success as a testament to faith. Kai exemplified fearlessness and courage in expressing his gratitude to God, showing his audience that true victory comes when we acknowledge the source of our strength.

THE RICH YOUNG RULER: A BIBLICAL REFLECTION

The story of the rich young ruler, found in the Gospels, offers a contrasting perspective. This man approached Jesus, asking what he must do to inherit eternal life. Despite his wealth and moral uprightness, he struggled to fully surrender his worldly possessions and trust in God. His attachment to his status and material success ultimately held him back from embracing the greater purpose Jesus called him to.

In contrast, Kai Cenat's journey shows what it looks like to prioritize faith over the world's expectations. Kai's willingness to openly celebrate God's role in his success demonstrates the courage the rich young ruler lacked. Kai's story reminds us that victories are most meaningful when they are rooted in gratitude and purpose rather than mere worldly recognition.

SHARED LESSONS OF RESILIENCE AND FAITH

Kai Cenat and the rich young ruler's stories provide valuable insights for overcoming the fear of failure and embracing faith:

1. COURAGE OVER CONFORMITY:

The rich young ruler conformed to societal values, prioritizing his wealth and status. Kai, on the other hand, boldly proclaimed his faith, showing that success is amplified when rooted in gratitude to God.

2. FEARLESSNESS IN FAITH:

The rich young ruler's fear of letting go contrasts with Kai's courage to give glory to God in a highly visible way. Kai's celebration reminds us that true success involves acknowledging and trusting in God's guidance.

3. ALIGNING WITH PURPOSE:

While the rich young ruler walked away from his calling, Kai embraced his platform as an opportunity to inspire others and glorify God, demonstrating how resilience and faith can turn setbacks into stepping stones.

RELATABILITY FOR COLLEGE STUDENTS

The stories of Kai Cenat and the rich young ruler resonate deeply with college students navigating their own fears and aspirations. Many students feel torn between societal pressures to achieve material success and the call to live authentically in alignment with their faith. Kai's example shows that it's possible to excel in the world while remaining true to one's spiritual values.

The rich young ruler's hesitation is a cautionary tale for students who might feel tempted to prioritize fleeting achievements over lasting purpose. Kai's story, on the other hand, inspires confidence in expressing faith, even in the face of societal norms that discourage it.

GOD'S GRACE IN OUR VICTORIES

Both Kai Cenat's celebration and the rich young ruler's struggle highlight an essential truth: success is most fulfilling when it is rooted in God's grace. Kai's openness about his faith demonstrates that courage and gratitude can inspire others to pursue their own spiritual journeys. The rich young ruler's story serves as a reminder that worldly success alone is never enough to satisfy the soul.

TURNING SETBACKS INTO STEPPING STONES

Every great story of success involves moments of failure and decisions about what truly matters. Kai Cenat's boldness in praising God after his victory and the rich young ruler's struggle to prioritize faith remind us that overcoming the fear of failure involves more than just perseverance—it requires aligning with purpose and courageously expressing gratitude to God.

When you feel overwhelmed or uncertain, remember Kai's breakthrough and the lesson of the rich young ruler. Trust that God's plan for your life includes every misstep and victory, using them to prepare you for greater things. Success isn't about avoiding failure; it's about rising above it and living out your faith boldly.

AFFIRM IT AGAIN

"I embrace the challenges before me and trust that every setback is a step toward the success God has destined for me."

LET'S FACE IT ACTIVITY

Think about a time when you faced a challenge that felt like a setback. Reflect on how it impacted you and what you learned from the experience. What would you do differently now with the perspective of faith?

....

....

....

....

....

....

....

Challenge

Create a short reel or TikTok sharing an inspiring moment where you turned a setback into a success. Use the hashtag #SetbacksToSteppingStones and tag your friends to encourage them to share their stories too.

Fearless Focus (Reflection)

1

Consider what setbacks you've faced recently. How might those experiences be preparing you for a greater purpose?

....

....

....

....

....

....

2

Reflect on the rich young ruler's story. Are there attachments or fears you need to surrender to live out God's plan for your life?

....

....

....

....

....

....

3

Write one actionable step to align your goals with God's purpose this week.

....

....

....

....

....

....

Remember This

1. Fear of failure can be transformed into a pathway to success through faith.

2. Gratitude to God amplifies victories and inspires others.

3. Success aligned with God's purpose is more fulfilling than worldly achievements.

4. Courage in expressing faith encourages others to embrace their spiritual journey.

Just like moons and like suns,
With the certainty of tides,
Just like hopes springing high,
Still I'll rise.

...

Out of the huts of history's shame
I rise

Up from a past that's rooted in pain
I rise

I'm a black ocean, leaping and wide,
Welling and swelling I bear in the tide.

Leaving behind nights of terror and fear
I rise

Into a daybreak that's wondrously clear
I rise

POEM EXCERPT FROM STILL I RISE
BY MAYA ANGELOU

CONQUERING THE VOICE OF DOUBT - OVERCOMING THE FEAR OF REJECTION

AFFIRM IT

"I am worthy of love and acceptance just as I am. I can rise above rejection!"

The fear of rejection can feel overwhelming, especially for students navigating the social challenges of transitioning into or out of high school and college. Whether it's not being accepted by a friend group, a dating interest, or not getting the grade or internship you aimed for, rejection can sting. But here's the truth: rejection is not the end. In fact, it can be a catalyst for your greatest growth and resilience.

Joseph, one of the greatest comeback figures of the Bible, is a powerful example of someone who faced rejection but ultimately triumphed. As a young man, Joseph was favored by God and his father, Jacob. He caught glimpses in the form of dreams about how successful he'd be when he grew up. He was gifted with a colorful coat, but this special treatment made those around him jealous. Their envy grew to the point that they rejected him entirely, selling him into slavery and making-up a story about his death. For Joseph, this betrayal must have been deeply painful. Yet, even in the pit while sinking into the realest depths of rejection, Joseph's story didn't end there.

Through every trial he faced—being sold into slavery, falsely accused, and imprisoned—Joseph remained faithful and resilient. God's favor was upon him, and he rose to prominence in Egypt, eventually becoming second in command under Pharaoh. When famine struck, Joseph's wisdom and leadership not only saved Egypt but also his own family, the very people who had rejected him. Instead of allowing bitterness to consume him, Joseph chose forgiveness and purpose, transforming rejection into restoration. His story reminds us that even in the face of betrayal and exclusion, God's plan for our lives can prevail.

Similarly, Maya Angelou, one of the most influential voices of the 20th century, knew what it felt like to face rejection. As a young, aspiring writer and performer, she was often told that her voice, her stories, and even her appearance did not fit the mold of what was "acceptable" in society at the time. Yet, instead of shrinking under the weight of rejection, she continued to rise. Her poetry, filled with truth, resilience, and confidence in her creative identity, reflected her refusal to let the rejection of others dictate her worth. Despite being told "no" many times, she became a symbol of perseverance and strength.

Angelou's journey, like Joseph's, shows us that rejection can never take away your worth unless you allow it to. Rejection is not a reflection of your value or potential; it's simply part of the process of life. When you look at rejection through a different lens, you realize it's not a closed door but an invitation to find another path—one that might lead you to an even better opportunity.

Overcoming the fear of rejection involves changing how you respond to it. To be completely honest, even Maya Angelou's story wasn't an immediate triumph over rejection and fear. She experienced a time in her life where the fear did win. After a traumatic experience as a child, she was literally silent for almost five years. The trauma left her feeling vulnerable and fearful of the world around her, leading her to believe that her voice would only bring pain. Yet, during this period of silence, she developed a profound appreciation for language and storytelling. When she finally found her voice again, it emerged with incredible power and authenticity, enabling her to inspire others and rise above the limitations that had once held her back.

Both Joseph and Maya Angelou teach us that rejection is not the end of the story. Whether it comes from family, society, or other external pressures, rejection is only a chapter—not the whole book. When we rely on God's guidance, like Joseph did, and draw strength from within, as Maya Angelou did, we can rise above rejection and continue pushing forward, confident that our worth is not tied to others' approval.

FACE YOUR FEARS ACTIVITY

Creative Writing Challenge: Your Story of Rising Above Rejection

1

Write about a time when you experienced rejection. How did it make you feel at first?

....

....

....

....

2

Now, imagine you're talking to your future self five years from now. Write an encouraging letter to yourself about how you rose above that rejection and how it helped you become stronger and more confident in who you are.

....

....

....

....

....

....

Challenge

Record yourself reading the letter or share a portion of it as a post on social media. You can even make it into a short poem. Use the hashtag #FearlessRejection2024 and inspire others to rise above their own challenges!

Fearless Mindset

Rejection is not the end; it's a stepping stone toward growth and new opportunities. Your worth is not determined by the approval of others. Like Joseph and Maya Angelou, you can rise above rejection and use it as fuel for your journey and inspire millions of other people in the process.

Fearless Focus (Reflection)

How does rejection make you feel, and what can you learn from it?

....

....

....

2

What are some ways you can respond differently to rejection moving forward?

....

....

....

3

How can you begin seeing rejection as an opportunity rather than a setback?

....

....

....

Remember This

1. Rejection is a part of the process, but it doesn't have to define you. Like Joseph, you can rise, face the challenges, and continue moving forward with confidence.

2. Every "no" gets you one step closer to the "yes" that's meant for you.

3. Rise above fear, and embrace the power within you to keep pushing forward, no matter what..

"Shoot for the moon. Even if you miss it, you will land among the stars. Don't let someone else's opinion of you become your reality. If you take responsibility for yourself, you will develop a hunger to accomplish your dreams."

LES BROWN

CHAPTER 3

STEPPING INTO GREATNESS WITHOUT HESITATION - OVERCOMING THE FEAR OF SUCCESS

AFFIRM IT

"I Am Ready to Embrace My Success. I don't have to fear the responsibility; I can enjoy the journey!"

SCAN TO VIEW VIDEO

Success can be a daunting prospect, often accompanied by an overwhelming fear that holds many back. This fear is not just about the pressure to perform; it can also stem from the responsibility that comes with growth. Many people, especially young adults, experience a paradoxical fear of success that keeps them from pursuing their true potential. Instead of dreaming big, they become paralyzed by the thought of what might happen if they actually achieve their goals.

This fear is often rooted in the worry of disappointing others or, conversely, fearing that success might lead to a loss of relationships or support systems. When someone begins to stand out or excel, it can trigger insecurities in others, leading to feelings of jealousy or resentment. This can create a toxic environment where success feels more like a burden than a blessing as we just learned about Joseph in our last chapter.

Mali Music, a Grammy Award-winning producer, singer, and songwriter, reflects on this tension as he grew in success. In his interview with The Certified Man Podcast Host KD Bowe, he reflects, "I had to learn that God's timing is perfect, and success is not about me but about being obedient to what He's called me to do." His words remind us that success isn't just about achieving goals; it's about aligning our journey with God's purpose for our lives. Mali began playing piano at 5 years old and singing prophetically at his church as the Minister of Music at just 11 years old, but his path wasn't without challenges. He had to overcome doubts, pressures, and the weight of expectations to become the impactful artist he is today.

The fear of success is not a new concept. The Bible tells us about Jeremiah, a prophet called by God at a young age. Jeremiah's success as a prophet was extraordinary, yet he faced immense opposition and self-doubt. When God first called him, Jeremiah protested, saying, "I do not know how to speak; I am too young" (Jeremiah 1:6 NIV). God's response was clear: "Do not say, 'I am too young.' You must go to everyone I send you to and say whatever I command you. Do not be afraid of them, for I am with you and will rescue you" (Jeremiah 1:7-8 NIV).

Jeremiah's story reminds us that God equips us for the assignments He gives us. Success doesn't mean we have to have all the answers or be perfect; it means trusting God's plan and stepping out in faith, even when it feels overwhelming. Like Mali Music, Jeremiah had to embrace God's timing and the responsibility at a young age that came with his calling, learning to navigate success with humility and courage.

The fear of success often intertwines with the fear of failure. Many individuals think that if they succeed, they must maintain that level of achievement indefinitely, leading to anxiety about future performance. It's crucial to recognize that success is not a permanent state; it's a series of milestones. Accepting that there will be ups and downs in the journey can help alleviate some of that pressure.

Moreover, as individuals achieve success, they may feel the weight of expectations from themselves and those around them. They might grapple with the ancient proverb: "To whom much is given, much is required." This idea can create an internal conflict where the fear of responsibility becomes too much. The good news is that embracing success means also embracing the idea of growth and learning. It's okay to stumble along the way; what matters is the courage to rise again and move forward.

Ultimately, overcoming the fear of success involves a mindset shift. By viewing success as an opportunity to impact others positively, individuals can change their relationship with success. It's not about being perfect; it's about being authentic and committed to personal growth. The success of your personal growth then ultimately impacts others around you.

LET'S FACE IT ACTIVITY: "SUCCESS INTERVIEWS/ ACCEPTANCE SPEECH"

OBJECTIVE

Engage in conversations to explore the fear of success and how to overcome it through insights from others.

INSTRUCTIONS

1. **Partner Up:** Form pairs with another student. If the group is large, you can do small groups of three.

2. **Interview Each Other (on-camera):** Each student will take turns interviewing their partner. Use the following questions to guide the conversation:

   - What personal achievement are you most proud of, and how did you overcome any fears or obstacles to reach it? (What award are you accepting today)

   - Who has inspired you in your journey toward success, and what lessons have you learned from them?

3. **Share Insights:** After the interviews, each student will summarize their partner's insights with the larger group or play their video.

Challenge

Write down three goals you've been hesitant to pursue because of fear. Take one intentional step toward achieving one of them this week.

1

....

2

....

3

....

Fearless Mindset

Success is not just about achieving milestones; it's about trusting God's timing, embracing the responsibility of growth, and staying authentic in the process. Like Jeremiah and Mali Music, you can overcome the fear of success by focusing on the journey rather than the destination and using your platform to inspire and uplift others.

Focus & Reflect

Take a moment to reflect on your thoughts and feelings regarding success. Write down your responses to the following prompts:

1

What does success mean to you?

....

....

....

....

....

2

What fears do you have about achieving success?

....

....

....

....

....

....

3

How can you reframe your perspective on success to view it as a positive journey?

....

....

....

....

....

....

4

What small steps can you take today to move closer to your goals?

....

....

....

....

....

....

Did you hear about the rose

that grew from a crack in the concrete?

Provin nature's laws wrong

it learned how to walk without havin feet

Funny it seems but, by keepin its dreams

It, learned to breathe FRESH air

Long live the rose that grew from concrete.

- TUPAC SHUKUR & GIOVANNI

CHAPTER 4

EMBRACING THE NEW YOU — OVERCOMING CHANGE & UNCERTAINTY

AFFIRM IT

"I am capable of transforming my circumstances, knowing that even the impossible can become possible with courage and determination."

SCAN TO VIEW VIDEO

Change is something that happens to everyone, but it can be really scary. For many students in high school and college, the idea of change makes one feel anxious and uncertain. Whether it's moving to a new school, adjusting to a different group of friends, going from off-campus to on-campus housing, or facing a major life transition, change can feel overwhelming. The fear of change often comes from not knowing what to expect. But it's important to remember that change is a normal part of life, and it can lead to exciting opportunities when you embrace the challenge.

Graduating from one level of school to the next is a big change that brings lots of mixed emotions. For example, going from high school to college or moving from one college to another can make even the most prepared person feel nervous and unsure of themselves. There's pressure to do well academically, make new friends, and adapt to a different environment. But these moments of change can also help you grow as a person and discover who you really are.

The Bible introduces us to an extraordinary young woman named Esther, who had to navigate overwhelming change and uncertainty. Esther was a Jewish girl living in Persia who suddenly found herself chosen to become the queen. This was a massive transition, not just in her daily life, but in the weight of responsibility placed on her shoulders. As queen, Esther discovered that her people were in danger of being wiped out due to a decree issued by Haman, a high-ranking official.

Imagine how uncertain and afraid Esther must have felt. She was living in a palace, away from her family and community, and now faced with the decision to risk her life by approaching the king without being summoned—a move that could lead to her execution. Yet, with encouragement from her cousin Mordecai, Esther embraced her new role and rose to the challenge. She said, "If I perish, I perish," and boldly took a stand for her people. Her courage and faith led to the salvation of the Jewish people and proved that even in the face of great uncertainty, God's plan can work through us.

One of the most important changes I experienced was when I decided to study abroad at Oxford University for five weeks during my senior semester while studying at Southern Wesleyan University for my Bachelor's degree. At first, the idea of living in another country and attending one of the top schools in the world, with people I did not know, made me feel anxious. I was worried about being away from home and having to meet new people. But I knew that stepping outside my comfort zone could lead to amazing experiences. When I arrived, I found myself surrounded by students from all over the world. I attended classes, joined discussions, and explored a new culture, which changed my view on life in ways I couldn't have imagined.

Studying at Oxford taught me that embracing change can lead to incredible life-changing opportunities. The fear I felt before leaving was replaced by excitement as I got involved in my classes and made friends from different backgrounds. I learned that facing uncertainty can help us grow stronger and more confident. Like Esther, who leaned on her faith and courage to overcome her fears, we too can rise to the occasion and embrace change with determination.

Overcoming the fear of change means seeing it as a chance to learn and grow. By accepting change, we open ourselves up to become more adaptable and resilient. To make the most of changes in your life, try setting small, achievable goals. For example, you might introduce yourself to someone new in class or join a club that interests you. Celebrate each little victory, as these small steps lead to bigger changes.

Esther's story and my own experience remind us that change is not something to fear; it's an opportunity to trust God and grow into the person He created you to be. When we embrace change with faith and determination, we can rise above any obstacle, just like the rose that grew from concrete.

LET'S FACE IT ACTIVITY:

Start a "**Change Journal**." Each time you face a change, write about it—how it made you feel, how you reacted, and what you learned from the experience. This will help you notice patterns in how you respond and allow you to handle future changes more effectively.

Challenge

List three changes you're currently facing or will face soon. Write one action step for each change that will help you navigate it positively.

Fearless Mindset

"I am capable of transforming my circumstances, knowing that even the impossible can become possible with courage and determination."

Fearless Focus (Reflection)

Think about a recent change you went through.

1

How did it affect you?

....

....

....

....

2

What did you learn from it?

....

....

....

....

....

....

....

3

How can Esther's story inspire you to trust God during uncertain times?

....

....

....

....

....

....

....

....

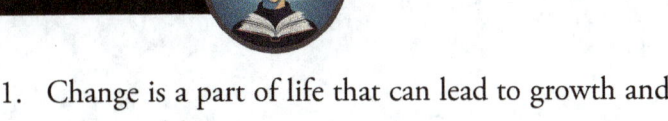

Remember This

1. Change is a part of life that can lead to growth and new opportunities.

2. Shifting your perspective on change can help you see it as a chance to thrive.

3. Everyone experiences fear of change; what matters is how you respond to it.

We lay down our arms
so we can reach out our arms to one another.

We seek harm to none and harmony for all.

Let the globe, if nothing else, say this is true.

That even as we grieved, we grew.

That even as we hurt, we hoped;
that even as we tired, we tried;
that we'll forever be tied together, victorious.

Not because we will never again know defeat,
but because we will never again sow division.

Scripture tells us to envision
that everyone shall sit under their own vine and fig tree,
and no one shall make them afraid.

If we're to live up to our own time,
then victory won't lie in the blade,
but in all the bridges we've made.

That is the promise to glade,
the hill we climb if only we dare it.

Because being American is more than a pride we inherit;
it's the past we step into and how we repair it.

EXCERPT FROM AMANDA GORMAN
"THE HILL WE CLIMB"

CHAPTER 5

UNINVITING THE IMPOSTER SYNDROME — OVERCOMING THE FEAR OF INADEQUACY

AFFIRM IT

"I am capable. I am able to. I am favored to. I am chosen to."

SCAN TO VIEW VIDEO

Have you ever felt like you're not enough, even when others say you're doing great? Maybe you've wondered if you truly deserve the opportunities or achievements you've earned. If so, you're not alone. This unsettling feeling is often described as "imposter syndrome." It's that nagging voice in your head that whispers, "You don't belong here," or, "You're not as good as everyone thinks you are."

Imposter syndrome can affect anyone—from students struggling with grades to accomplished professionals at the top of their game. You might look around at your peers and think, "They have it all together, while I'm just trying to keep up." But here's the truth: Even the most successful people often feel like imposters.

Let's consider a moment in history that captivated the world: Amanda Gorman, a young poet, stood on the steps of the U.S. Capitol and delivered her powerful inaugural poem, "The Hill We Climb." In it, she declared:

"There is always light, if only we're brave enough to see it. If only we're brave enough to be it."

Amanda Gorman, like many of us, has spoken openly about battling self-doubt. She has a speech impediment that made her feel inadequate at times, yet she stood boldly, embodying courage and brilliance as the youngest inaugural poet in U.S. history. Her story is a reminder that even when you feel inadequate, bravery can help you rise above fear and fulfill your purpose.

Similarly, the Bible tells the story of **Gideon**, who also battled feelings of inadequacy. When God called Gideon to deliver Israel from the Midianites, Gideon's immediate reaction was one of doubt. He said, "But Lord, how can I save Israel? *My clan is the weakest in Manasseh, and I am the least in my family*" (Judges 6:15). Yet, God saw Gideon's potential and reassured him, saying, "*I will be with you*" (Judges 6:16). With faith and God's guidance, Gideon overcame his fears and led Israel to victory, proving that God equips those He calls.

What can we learn from Amanda Gorman and Gideon? Both faced overwhelming odds and inner doubts, but they stepped into their calling with courage and faith. Overcoming imposter syndrome begins with recognizing that your feelings of inadequacy do not define you.

When self-doubt creeps in, take a moment to reflect on your strengths and accomplishments. My mentor calls this your "Trophy Case." Write down your achievements—big or small— and revisit them when you need a reminder of your capability. Did you ace a tough exam? Add it to the list. Did you step out of your comfort zone in any way? Celebrate it. These reminders help combat the lies imposter syndrome tells you.

Amanda Gorman once said, "Poetry is for everyone," a statement that encourages us to believe that our unique gifts and voices matter. Like her, you are capable of climbing your own hill, no matter how steep it seems. And like Gideon, you can overcome fear by trusting in God's promises and stepping into your purpose.

When imposter syndrome tries to tell you otherwise, remember this: God doesn't call the qualified; He qualifies the called. Your path is uniquely yours, and no amount of self-doubt can take away the potential God has placed within you.

LET'S FACE IT ACTIVITY

Your "**Trophy Case.**" Write down at least 10 achievements or milestones you're proud of. Keep this list somewhere accessible so you can revisit it whenever you feel inadequate.

Challenge

Identify one area of your life where you feel like an imposter. Take one bold step this week to combat that feeling, like volunteering for a leadership role, asking for help, or sharing your ideas in a group setting.

Fearless Mindset

"I am chosen, prepared, and equipped to fulfill my God-given purpose. Self-doubt has no place in my story."

Fearless Focus (Reflection)

Think of a time when you doubted your abilities but succeeded anyway.

1

What did you learn from that experience?

....

....

....

....

....

2

How does Amanda Gorman's courage or Gideon's faith inspire you to keep going?

....

....

....

....

....

Remember This

1. Imposter syndrome is a feeling, not your reality.

2. God sees your potential, even when you don't.

3. Bravery, faith, and action can silence self-doubt and open doors to your purpose.

Maybe we are all just frightened to stand out
knowing that on platforms

we represent something greater
but only our imperfections

seem to be so appealing to spectators
people may pick apart every flaw that can be seen
and diminish our confidence

so that their inadequacy becomes invisible.

So for now, forget peripherals and let's focus on 3 things:

One, Fear knows that normality is a nuisance;
a rope that chokes your boldness so that you think that
you are useless.

Two, Mediocrity, that's just Ludacris.

I'm only fearful of blending into the crowd because
I'm not sure that life won't overlook me, if I bear
resemblance to everyone else around me.

Three, Conformity makes you a traditionalist. Stop being
so afraid and try being fearless.

EXCERPT FROM THE FEARLESS POEM
BY JAYE SMITH

CHAPTER 6

FINDING YOUR VOICE — OVERCOMING THE FEAR OF PUBLIC SPEAKING

AFFIRM IT

"I am capable of handling my responsibilities while honoring my true self."

SCAN TO VIEW VIDEO

Public speaking is often described as one of the greatest fears people face, even more daunting than visible dangers. Many of us experience that overwhelming anxiety when faced with speaking in front of a crowd. Whether it's giving a class presentation, sharing ideas in a meeting, or speaking at a special event, the fear of public speaking can keep you from sharing your ideas and reaching your full potential.

This fear often stems from worrying about judgment or making mistakes. Thoughts like, "What if I forget my words?" or "What if I embarrass myself?" can paralyze even the most prepared person. But stepping into this fear is a powerful step toward personal growth and leadership.

Let's take inspiration from someone who has overcome the challenges of public speaking: Tim Tebow, a professional athlete and Christian role model. Tebow has shared his faith and personal experiences with audiences worldwide, often facing criticism for being so open about his beliefs. Despite this, he has consistently spoken with conviction and humility. Tebow once said, "Success is not about how much money you make; it's about the difference you make in people's lives." His commitment to inspiring others has helped him navigate the pressure and fear of public speaking, proving that courage comes from focusing on the message, not the fear.

Similarly, the Bible tells us about Moses, a man who also struggled with the fear of speaking. When God called Moses to lead the Israelites out of Egypt, Moses hesitated. He said, "Pardon your servant, Lord. I have never been eloquent...I am slow of speech and tongue" (Exodus 4:10). Moses doubted his ability to speak before Pharaoh and lead a nation. But God reassured him, saying, "Now go; I will help you speak and will teach you what to say" (Exodus 4:12). With God's guidance—and the support of his brother Aaron—Moses found his voice and became one of history's greatest leaders.

What can we learn from Tim Tebow and Moses? Both faced fear and doubt about their ability to speak, yet they stepped forward with faith and determination. They remind us that finding your voice isn't about perfection; it's about trusting the purpose behind your words and the impact they can have.

STRATEGIES TO OVERCOME PUBLIC SPEAKING ANXIETY

1. PREPARE THOROUGHLY

The more you know your topic, the more confident you'll feel. Outline your speech, make notes, and practice diligently.

2. PRACTICE REGULARLY

Start rehearsing early, and practice in front of family or friends to build confidence and receive feedback.

3. VISUALIZE SUCCESS

Picture yourself speaking confidently, connecting with your audience, and receiving their positive reactions.

4. FOCUS ON YOUR MESSAGE

Concentrate on the value of what you're sharing instead of worrying about how you'll be perceived.

5. EMBRACE MISTAKES

Understand that even seasoned speakers make mistakes. Acknowledge them, laugh it off, and keep going.

6. CONNECT WITH YOUR AUDIENCE

Share personal stories or experiences to create a connection. It makes your speech more engaging and relatable.

LET'S FACE IT ACTIVITY:

Prepare a 2-minute speech about a topic you're passionate about, such as a hobby, a cause you care about, or a personal story. Practice in front of a friend or family member and ask for feedback.

Challenge : #FearlessSpeech

After completing the "Let's Face It" activity, take your public speaking practice a step further:

1. **Record Your Speech:** Deliver your prepared 2-minute speech on a topic you're passionate about. Aim for a concise 60-90 second version suitable for a social media reel.

2. **Share with #FearlessSpeech:** Post your video on your preferred social media platform using the hashtag #FearlessSpeech.

3. **Encourage Engagement:** Invite friends and peers to watch your reel, provide constructive feedback, and share their own #FearlessSpeech videos.

Focus & Reflect

Take a moment to write down your thoughts on the following prompts:

1

What makes you feel confident when speaking?

....

....

....

....

....

....

2

Describe a time when you overcame a fear of public speaking.

....

....

....

....

3

How can you support others in their public speaking journey?

....

....

....

....

4

What message do you want to share with the world?

....

....

....

....

Fearless Mindset

"I am confident that God is leading me step by step as I follow His plan and purpose for me, so I do not have to fear."

Remember This

1. Public speaking is a skill that improves with practice.

2. Fear is natural, but it can be channeled into positive energy.

3. Your voice is unique and powerful—use it to inspire and connect.

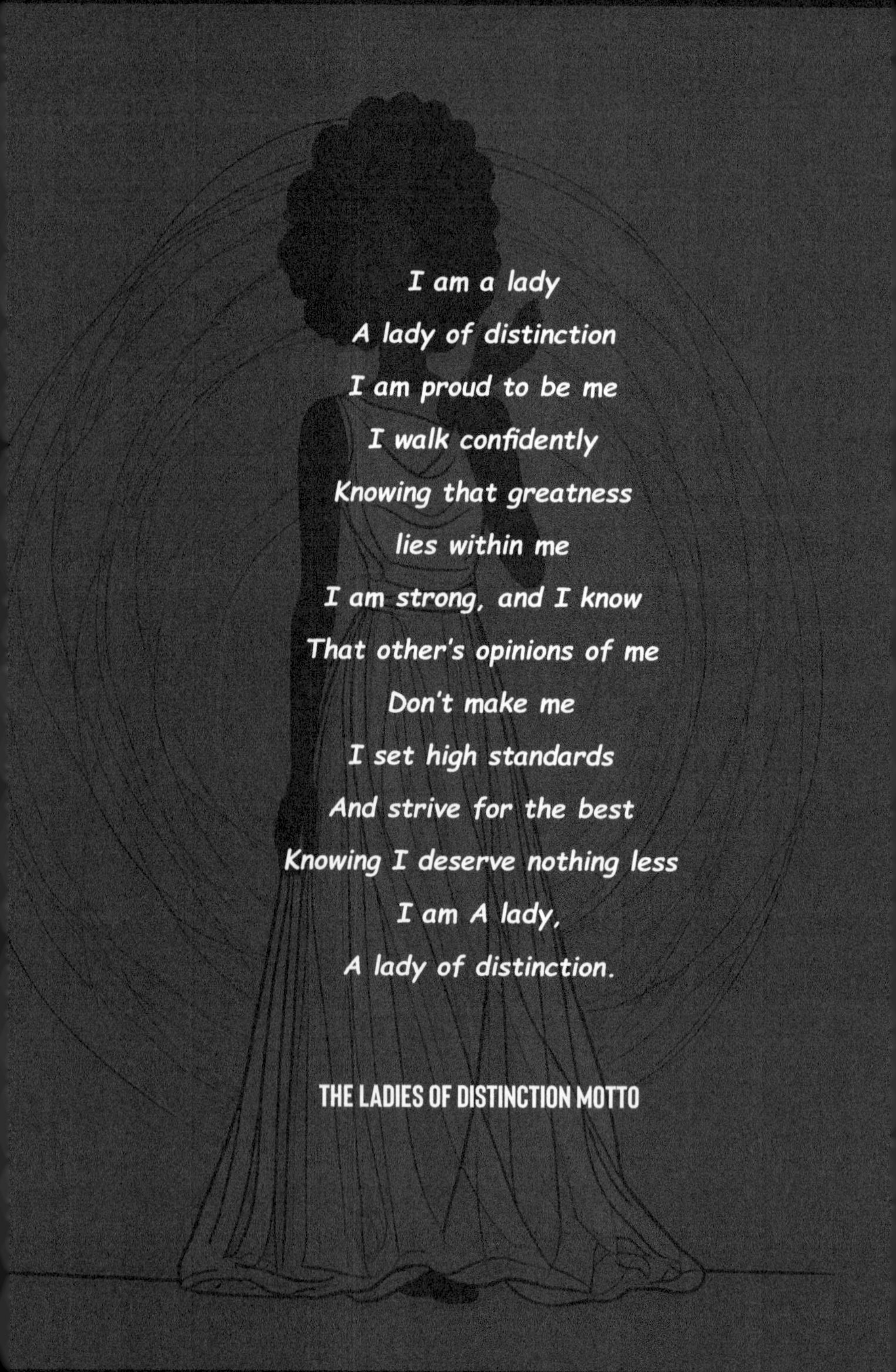

I am a lady

A lady of distinction

I am proud to be me

I walk confidently

Knowing that greatness

lies within me

I am strong, and I know

That other's opinions of me

Don't make me

I set high standards

And strive for the best

Knowing I deserve nothing less

I am A lady,

A lady of distinction.

THE LADIES OF DISTINCTION MOTTO

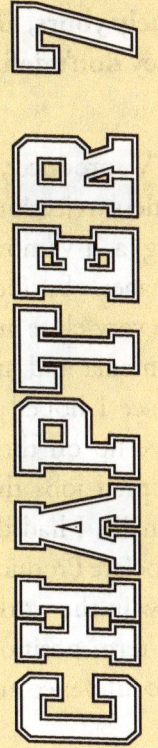

CHAPTER 7

DO IT FOR YOU — OVERCOMING THE FEAR OF LETTING OTHERS DOWN

AFFIRM IT

"I am strong, and I know that other's opinions of me, don't make me. "

SCAN TO VIEW VIDEO

Have you ever felt burdened by the fear of disappointing those you care about? The opinions of teachers, family, and friends can sometimes weigh so heavily that you find yourself prioritizing their expectations over your own goals and dreams. Yet, one of the most empowering lessons you can embrace is this: **your journey is uniquely yours, and while others' opinions may influence you, they don't define your purpose.**

During my pursuit of a dream job as a TV producer, I encountered numerous challenges and countless rejections. After ten years of persevering through being a TV/movie production intern, then social media manager, business owner, and multimedia video producer, I came very close and had wonderful life-changing opportunities in media and arts production, but I was still not quite at the place I hoped to be at the time. After revisiting the urge to give up on those dreams, I surrendered to the process and accepted jobs that developed my skills and portfolio over time. Finally, I had the opportunity to interview for a position as an Associate Producer with TBN, home to the #1 female-led faith show in the world, *Better Together*. Although I didn't secure a long-term position, the experience was invaluable; it bolstered my confidence and taught me vital lessons for my future endeavors.

Inspired by my journey, I dedicated myself to helping others achieve their dreams of breaking into TV/media production. I developed internships for students aspiring to enter media arts and entertainment, empowering the next generation by sharing my knowledge and offering them opportunities to shine. This was a direct result of my commitment to personal growth, developing authentic personal and professional relationships, helping others to bring their vision to life, and simultaneously overcoming the fear of letting others down.

Similarly, Ruth's story exemplifies the power of loyalty and purpose-driven actions. After a difficult loss, Ruth had the opportunity to return to her own family. Instead, she chose to stay with Naomi, her mother-in-law, and work alongside her as she always had. Ruth's faithfulness and dedication to Naomi went beyond familial duty—it was an act of purpose. Ruth declared, *"Where you go, I will go, and where you stay, I will stay. Your people will be my people, and your God my God."* (Ruth 1:16). Her loyalty eventually led her to Boaz, her future husband, and placed her in the lineage of King David and, ultimately, Jesus Christ.

Ruth's unwavering commitment to Naomi and her journey serves as a reminder that when we act in alignment with our purpose and remain true to our values, we can impact generations. Her story echoes the lesson I've learned: pursuing your passions and embracing your unique path not only benefits you but creates ripples that inspire and uplift others.

Overcoming the fear of letting others down begins with shifting your mindset. It's about focusing on who you want to become and allowing your journey to unfold authentically. Your growth and success are not just for you—they contribute to the lives of everyone around you. Like Ruth, you have the power to inspire and bless generations by staying true to your purpose.

LET'S FACE IT ACTIVITY:

1. **Self-Reflection:** Identify an area in your life where fear of disappointing others has held you back.

2. **Action Plan:** Write down a specific step to prioritize your own goals in this area, and set a timeline for completing it.

3. **Accountability:** Share your plan with a trusted friend or mentor to help hold you accountable.

Challenge

After completing the activity, create a 60-90 second video sharing your experience. Discuss the area you identified, the action you plan to take, and how you feel about prioritizing your own goals. Post your video on social media using the hashtag #FearlessFocus to inspire others to overcome their fears.

Fearless Focus

1

How do I define success for myself, independent of others' expectations?

....

....

....

....

....

....

2

What fears do I have about letting others down, and where do they come from?

....

....

....

....

....

....

3

How can I create a support system that encourages my personal growth?

....

....

....

....

....

....

4

Reflect on a time when prioritizing yourself led to a positive outcome. What did you learn from that experience?

....

....

....

....

....

....

Fearless Mindset

"I am confident and equipped to share my voice. My message matters, and I trust God to guide my words."

Remember This

1. Your self-worth is not defined by others' opinions; focus on your own goals and values.

2. Shift your mindset from doing things for approval to doing them for your true self.

3. Your growth and success have a positive impact on your community.

4. It's okay to fear letting others down, but don't let that fear hold you back.

If you can keep your head when all about you
Are losing theirs and blaming it on you;

If you can trust yourself when all men doubt you,
But make allowance for their doubting too;
If you can wait and not be tired by waiting,

Or being lied about, don't deal in lies,
Or being hated, don't give way to hating,
And yet don't look too good, nor talk too wise:

...

If you can force your heart and nerve and sinew
To serve your turn long after they are gone,

And so hold on when there is nothing in you
Except the Will which says to them: "Hold on!"

If you can talk with crowds and keep your virtue,
Or walk with kings—nor lose the common touch,
If neither foes nor loving friends can hurt you,

If all men count with you, but none too much;

If you can fill the unforgiving minute
With sixty seconds' worth of distance run,
Yours is the Earth and everything that's in it,
And—which is more—you'll be a Man, my son!

"IF" - BY RUDYARD KIPLING

HANG IN THERE — OVERCOMING THE FEAR OF COMMITMENT

AFFIRM IT

"I am confident in my ability to commit to my goals and trust the process to fulfill my purpose."

SCAN TO VIEW VIDEO

Commitment can often feel intimidating, especially for students who are still navigating their paths. For many, the idea of sticking to a decision—be it a college major, a career field, or a personal goal—can seem overwhelming. The fear of commitment often stems from uncertainty and the worry of making the wrong choice. Yet, commitment is not about perfection; it's about perseverance, growth, and trusting the process.

A powerful modern-day example of commitment comes from Michael Vick, former NFL quarterback turned head coach at Norfolk State University. After a storied career marked by both triumphs and setbacks, Vick's journey has become a testament to resilience and dedication. By committing to his new role, Vick has embraced the opportunity to mentor young athletes and give back to the community. His decision to step into leadership reflects a deeper understanding of how commitment can pave the way for growth and inspire others.

Similarly, in the Bible, David's story illustrates the rewards of steadfastness despite trials and delays. Anointed as king while still a young shepherd, David's journey to the throne was full of challenges, including being pursued by friends and foes. Yet, David's commitment to his calling never wavered. He trusted God's timing and remained faithful, ultimately fulfilling his destiny as one of Israel's greatest kings despite his many personal setbacks. His story reminds us that commitment is about faith and perseverance, even when the path seems uncertain.

Commitment is not just about reaching a specific destination; it's about embracing the journey. Like Michael Vick, who has transitioned from player to coach, and David, who remained faithful despite setbacks, our dedication to our goals can lead to opportunities we never imagined. Moreover, our commitment inspires those around us, creating a ripple effect that extends far beyond our immediate sphere.

When fear threatens to hold us back, we must remember that commitment is an act of faith. It's about believing in our ability to overcome obstacles and trusting that our hard work will yield results. By staying the course, we grow stronger, more resilient, and better equipped to handle life's challenges. Just as David's faithfulness prepared him to lead a nation, our persistence can prepare us for the roles we are destined to play.

LET'S FACE IT ACTIVITY

REFLECT AND PLAN

1. **Identify Your Commitment:** Reflect on a college, career path, or personal goal you've been hesitant to commit to.

2. **Acknowledge Support:** Consider the family members, friends, or mentors who have supported you in your journey.

3. **Encourage Others:** Think about a message you would share to inspire your peers to commit to their goals.

Take a few minutes to jot down your thoughts on these points. This reflection will prepare you for the upcoming challenge.

....

....

....

....

....

....

....

....

The Challenge

#ICOMMITTED SPEECH

1. **Record Your Video: Create a short video (60-90 seconds) where you:**

   ☐ Share Your Commitment: Clearly state the college, career field, or life goal you are committing to.

   ☐ Express Gratitude: Acknowledge and thank the family, friends, and mentors who have supported you.

   ☐ Inspire Your Peers: Conclude with an encouraging message motivating others to commit to their goals.

2. **Post and Engage:**

   ☐ Share on Social Media: Upload your video to your preferred social media platform.

   ☐ Use the Hashtag: Include the hashtag #ICommitted in your post.

   ☐ Tag Others: Mention friends or peers to encourage them to participate and share their own commitments.

Fearless Focus

1

What fears do I have about making a long-term commitment, and where do they stem from?

....

....

....

....

....

....

2

How can I reframe my mindset to see commitment as an opportunity rather than a burden?

....

....

....

....

....

....

3

Reflect on a time when I stayed committed to a goal. What did I learn from that experience?

....

....

....

....

....

....

....

....

....

....

The Challenge

Identify one goal or responsibility you've been hesitant to commit to fully. Write down a specific plan to take the first step toward that commitment, including a timeline for action. Share your plan with a trusted mentor or friend to hold yourself accountable.

Fearless Mindset

"I am confident and equipped to fulfill my commitments. My dedication inspires others, and I trust God to guide my path."

Remember This

1. Commitment is not about perfection; it's about perseverance and growth.

2. Your dedication to your goals can inspire and uplift others.

3. Trust the process and have faith in your ability to succeed.

YOU ARE READY TO SOAR!

As you conclude this journey, embrace the "Ready, Set, Soar" mindset, encapsulating the essence of Isaiah 60:1: "Arise, shine, for your light has come, and the glory of the Lord rises upon you." Each chapter has equipped you with tools and insights to navigate your path to success, empowering you to rise above challenges and fearlessly pursue your dreams with the right community to guide and help you on your journey.

READY: YOU KNOW YOUR WORTH

Your journey began with understanding your intrinsic value. Recognizing that you are worthy of your dreams and aspirations has allowed you to build a solid foundation for personal growth. You have learned that your self-worth is not defined by others' opinions but by your commitment to yourself.

SET: YOU OVERCAME YOUR FEARS

You acknowledged your fears and confronted them head-on. By facing the fear of judgment, disappointment, and failure, you have unlocked new opportunities and taken bold steps toward your goals.

SOAR: YOU LET GO OF EXTERNAL VALIDATION

To truly soar, you released the need for external validation. By prioritizing the pure pursuit of your own dreams and aspirations over the expectations of others, you have cultivated a mindset of authenticity and purpose. This journey is not selfish; it is about outgrowing a people-pleasing mentality and fostering personal growth that ultimately benefits those around you.

YOU COMMITTED: YOU FINISHED WHAT YOU STARTED

Commitment is crucial for long-term success. Embracing the dedication to finish what you start, you understand that your efforts today will impact your future and the futures of others. As you pursue your goals, remember that hard work pays off. Each step brings you closer to realizing your potential and making a meaningful difference in your community.

MAKE THE JUMP!

As you prepare to take off into your future, carry these key takeaways with you: You know your worth, have confronted your fears, let go of the need for approval, and committed to your goals. You are equipped to embrace your journey with confidence and determination.

Your story is unique, and the path ahead is yours to create. With each decision you make and every obstacle you overcome, you are not only growing but also inspiring those around you. Remember, the world is waiting for you to soar. So...

READY... SET... SOAR!

Thank you for allowing me to be part of your journey. I believe in you, and I can't wait to see how fearlessly you will soar as you pursue your dreams..

JASMINE M. SMITH

Jasmine M. Smith is a dynamic and passionate media and communications professional with a deep commitment to igniting fearless courage in others, particularly youth, to pursue their dreams in media, arts, and leadership. A 2013 graduate of Southern Wesleyan University with a bachelor of arts degree in Media Communications, Jasmine's academic journey has taken her to prestigious institutions such as Oxford University in England and The Los Angeles Film Studies Center in California. These formative experiences laid the foundation for her impressive career in media and digital marketing.

After relocating to Los Angeles in June 2013, Jasmine quickly immersed herself in the world of digital media production and marketing, working with some of the biggest names in Hollywood. Her early career experiences included collaborating with prominent producers at Releve Entertainment, known for productions like Preachers of L.A. and Fix My Choir, and Edmonds Entertainment, which produced the hit film Jumping The Broom. These opportunities allowed her to gain invaluable insights into the entertainment industry while honing her expertise in production, digital strategy and faith-celebrity brand development.

Jasmine's talents and passion for media and ministry opened doors for her to contribute to high-profile global outreach initiatives, such as the California Dreamin campaign by Harvest International Ministries. She also played a significant role in shaping the branding and marketing efforts for Faith-based nonprofits and organizations, demonstrating her ability to create impactful media strategies that resonate with diverse audiences.

In 2016, Jasmine launched her own media company, Envision Media, with a mission to develop media services and solutions for Christian organizations, small churches, and public figures. Through her company, she has consulted globally, helping clients in the entertainment and media sectors develop innovative digital media strategies. Her entrepreneurial spirit and commitment to excellence continue to shape her work in the entertainment and media industry.

Her career took another leap when she joined the digital department at CBN's 700 Club, a platform that further expanded her skills in digital media production. Additionally, Jasmine worked as a Freelance Associate Producer for TBN's popular show Better Together, showcasing her capacity to be a part of a leading team producing a daily syndicated talk show for a global audience reaching millions of homes daily.

Jasmine holds an M.A. in Strategic Communication from Regent University, is a Doctor of Strategic Leadership Candidate at Regent University's School of Business and Leadership, and is currently pursuing a Ph.D. in Strategic Media at Liberty University. Her academic and professional journey is complemented by her involvement in leadership development for young people. In 2020, she founded L.E.A.D. Youth, an internship and apprentice program under the Jewel L. Britt Scholarship Fund Inc., a 501c3 organization. L.E.A.D. provides resources, summer programs, and hands-on experiences to prepare aspiring media and arts professionals for college and future careers in leadership, entrepreneurship, arts, and design.

Through her vast experiences, Jasmine has become an emerging voice in media and student leadership, dedicated to equipping the next generation with the skills and courage to succeed. Her work and educational pursuits are a testament to her relentless drive to empower others and make a lasting impact in her field.